Favorite Recorder Tunes

Early Music Gems

Marcia Diehl

The Rottenburgh Baroque recorder model 4204 of boxwood on our cover is courtesy of Moeck Musikinstrumente + Verlag GmbH, Celle - Germany.

WWW.MELBAY.COM

Preface

This collection of *Early Music Gems* is intended for the soprano and tenor recorders.

The time span of these selections begins with compositions by Beatrice de Dia of the 12th century through the Renaissance to the early Baroque music by Giovanni Battista Pergolesi. Beatrice de Dia is of notable interest for she was a *trobairitz*, a female troubadour and composer, who wrote songs of courtly love, a rarity for her time period. Currently, there are only five of her compositions known to exist, so I've ended this collection with two of them as a nod to this significant trailblazer.

Guilliaume de Machaut's "Douce dame jolie" is mesmerizing in its haunting modal melody.

Many Renaissance dance tunes are included from the rich oeuvres of Michael Praetorius, Tielman Susato, Claude Gervaise, and John Playford. Since they were written for the purpose of dance, I suggest repeating the entire piece for the intended effect. A hand drum or tambourine accompaniment would make an authentic addition. Playford's "Italian Rant" is meant to accelerate with each repetition into a near frenzied state.

Englishman Thomas Morley, a contemporary of Shakespeare, added a wealth of madrigals to the genre. "It Was a Lover and His Lass" was thought to have been used in stage performances of *As You Like It* in London during the playwright's lifetime. "Wither Away So Fast?" is another spirited madrigal, a love song.

"Greensleeves" and "Drive the Cold Winter Away" are lovely melancholic ballads familiar to many.

This musical era is special to recorder players. It is quite special to me. I hope you enjoy exploring this compilation.

Marcia Diehl

Index

Branle

Guárdame las Vacas

Luis de Narváez

Now, Musicians, Come

Hans Leo Hassler

Drive the Cold Winter Away

for Carolyn

John Playford

Bourée

for Marj

Michael Praetorius

Hard by a Fountain

Hubert Waelrant

Saltarello

Vincenzo Galilei

Lacrimae Antiquae

John Dowland

Pavane

Claude Gervaise

Galliard

Claude Gervaise

♩ = 120

D A D

7 A Bm D A D A D

14 A Bm D

19 A D A

23 D Bm D A D A

29 D A Bm

Saltarello

Anonymous
14th c

♩. = 94

5

1.

9

2.

13

17

1.

21

2.

In Dulci Jubilo

Michael Praetorius

Ecco la Primavera

Francesco Landini

Allemande

Claude Gervaise

Philomela Lost Her Love

Thomas Morley

Greensleeves

Traditional

Nowell, Nowell, Tidings True

Anonymous
15th c

Ce fut en mai

Moniot d'Arras

Danserye No. 6

Tielman Susato

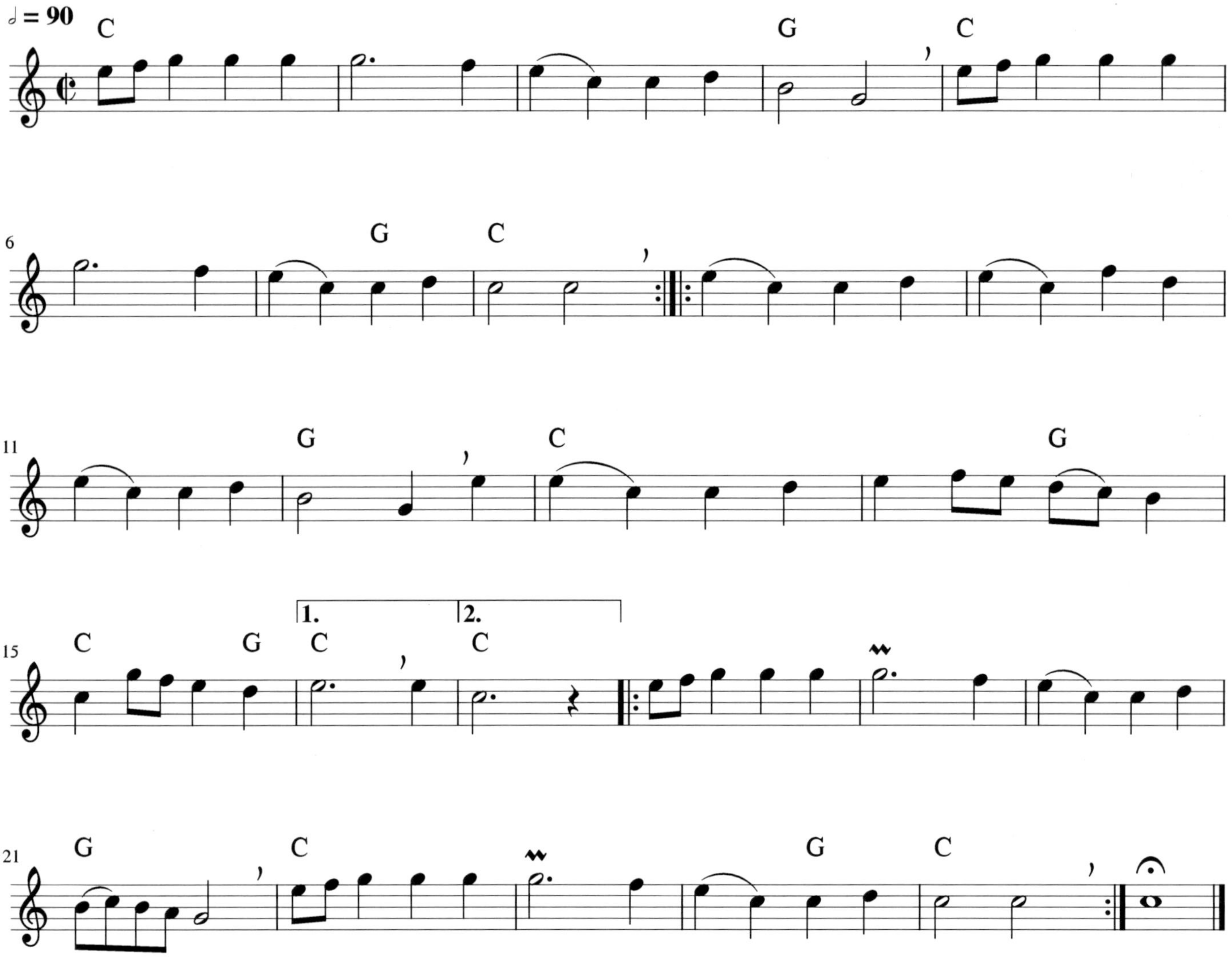

𝅗𝅥 = 90

C G C

6 G C

11 G C G

15 C G C C
1. 2.

21 G C G C

Danserye No. 18

Tielman Susato

Gavotte from Terpsichore

Michael Praetorius

𝅗𝅥 = 88

G Am G

7 C D G G C G C G

13 Am G D G Am G D G

18 Am G D G

24 C D G

29 C D G Am G

35 C D G Am G C D G

Torch Dance from Terpsichore

Michael Praetorius

Lamentatio

Ludwig Senfl

♩ = 112

C5 G5 F5 D5 G5 E5 F5

7 G5 C5 G5 D5 G5 F5 D5 G5

15 C5 D5 F5 G5 D5 G5

21 D5 F5 C5 G5 D5 A5

26 D5 A5 E5 D5 F5 G5 C5

Italian Rant
for Anita

John Playford

♩ = 144-160

Am Dm C G C G Am

5 C D Em G C

9 Am G Am

12 Dm C G C G Am

Alman

Robert Johnson

Basse danse

Anonymous
15th c

♩ = 94

A5 C5 E5 C5 E5

7 D5 A5 E5 G5

13 C5 F5 E5 A5 FIN G5

19 D5 E5 B5 D5 E5

25 A5 C5 E5 C5 E5

31 D5 A5 C5 A5

36 E5 C5 D5 A5 𝄋

The Cradle

Antony Holborne

Packington's Pound

Anonymous
16th c

Lo, How a Rose E'er Blooming

Michael Praetorius

Wither Away So Fast?

Thomas Morley

𝅗𝅥 = 72

C F C G F C D

7 Em Am Em Am G D

13 G F C A Dm C

18 G Am D G F

23 C G D C G Dm

28 Am G C F G D G

34 F Dm C G C D G

Mistress Mine

Francis Pilkington

Douce dame jolie

Guillaume de Machaut

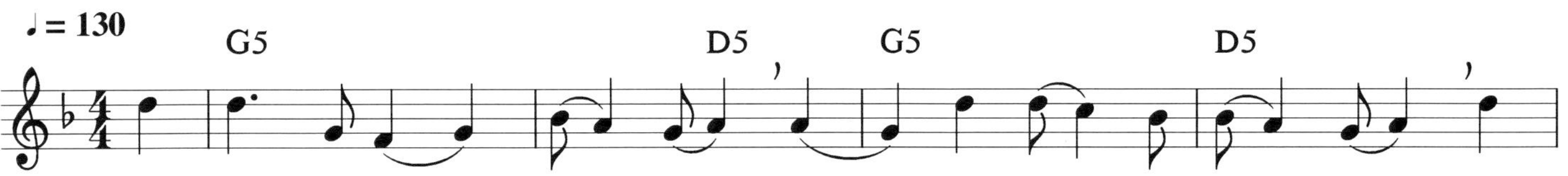

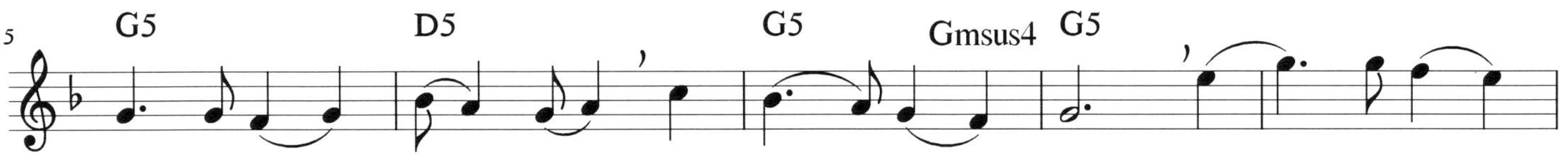

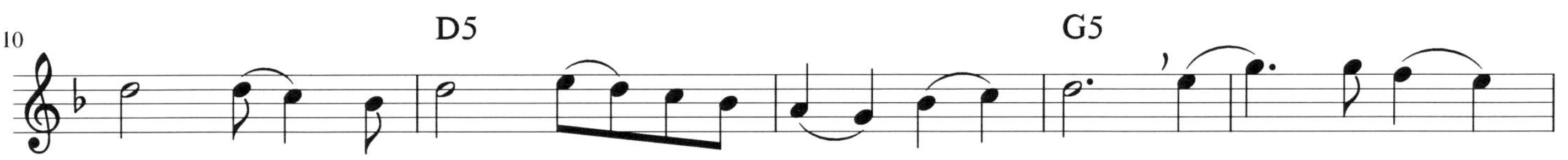

Trotto

Anonymous
13th c

Verily, Verily I Say Unto You

Thomas Tallis

♩ = 116

6

11

16

20

24

29

33

Les tendres souhaits

Giovanni Battista Pergolesi

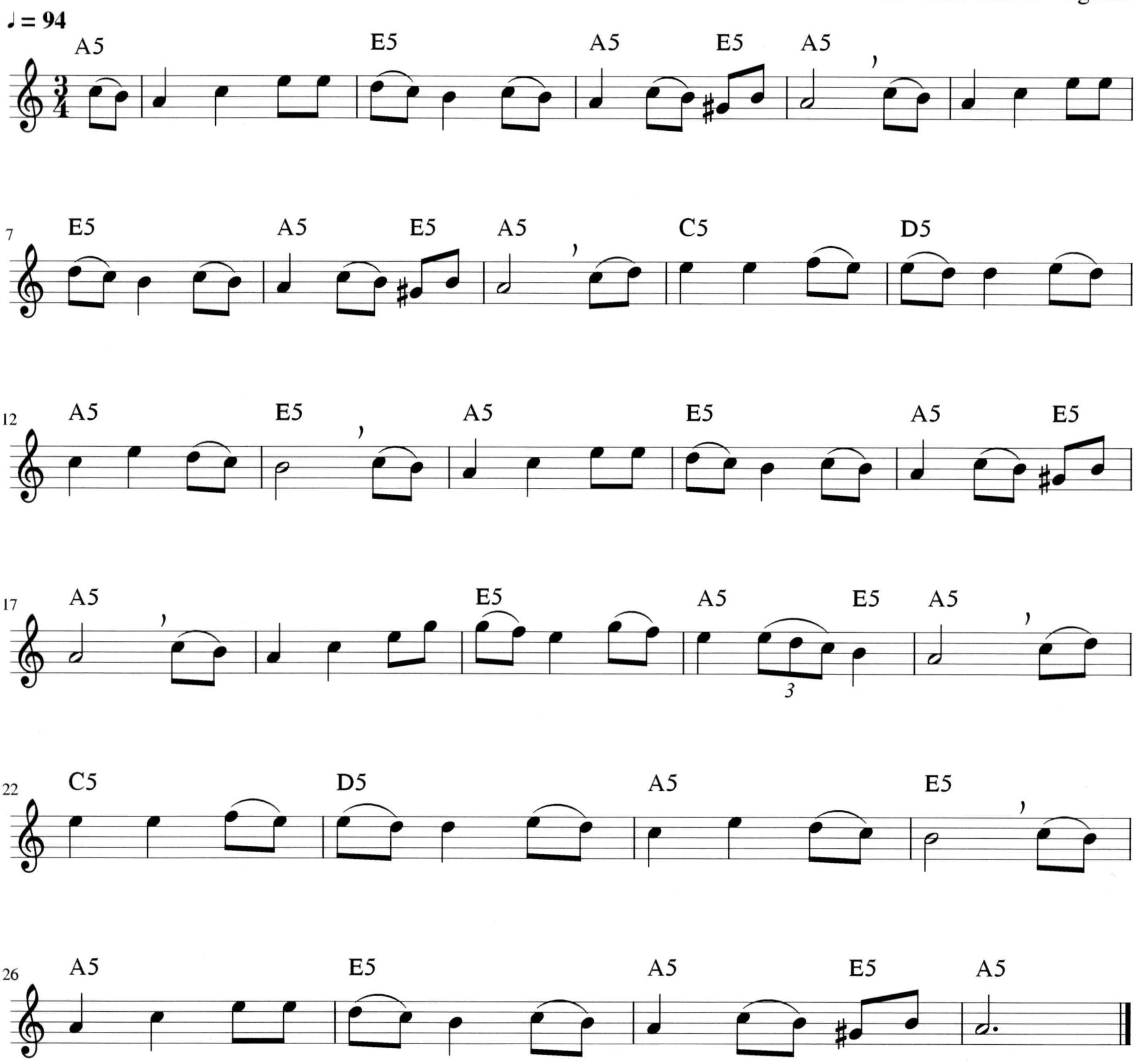
♩ = 94
A5 E5 A5 E5 A5
7 E5 A5 E5 A5 C5 D5
12 A5 E5 A5 E5 A5 E5
17 A5 E5 A5 E5 A5
3
22 C5 D5 A5 E5
26 A5 E5 A5 E5 A5

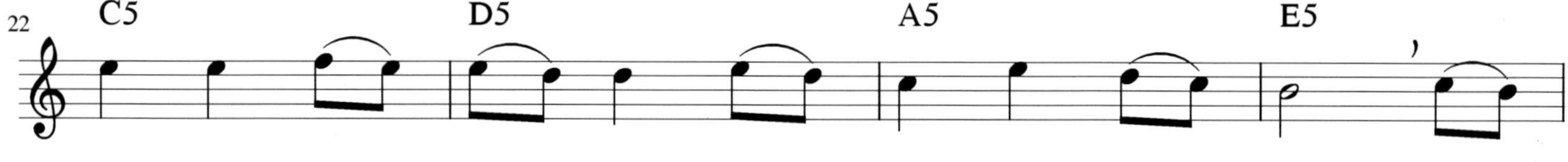

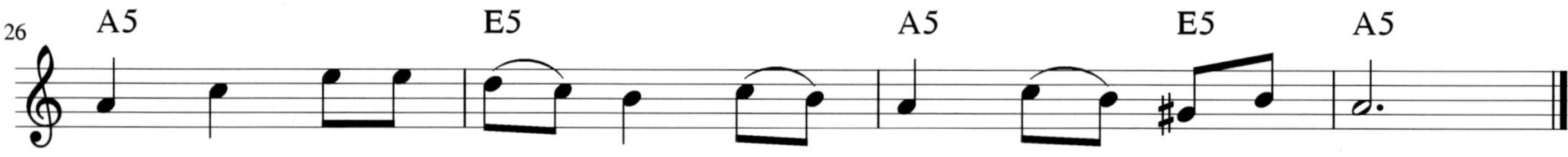

It Was a Lover and His Lass

for Dene

Thomas Morley

Prince Rupert Air and March

La Volta

William Byrd

Espagñoletas

Gaspar Sanz

Chanson d'amour

Beatriz de Dia

A chantar m'er de so qu'ieu non volria

Beatriz de Dia

♩ = 94

G5